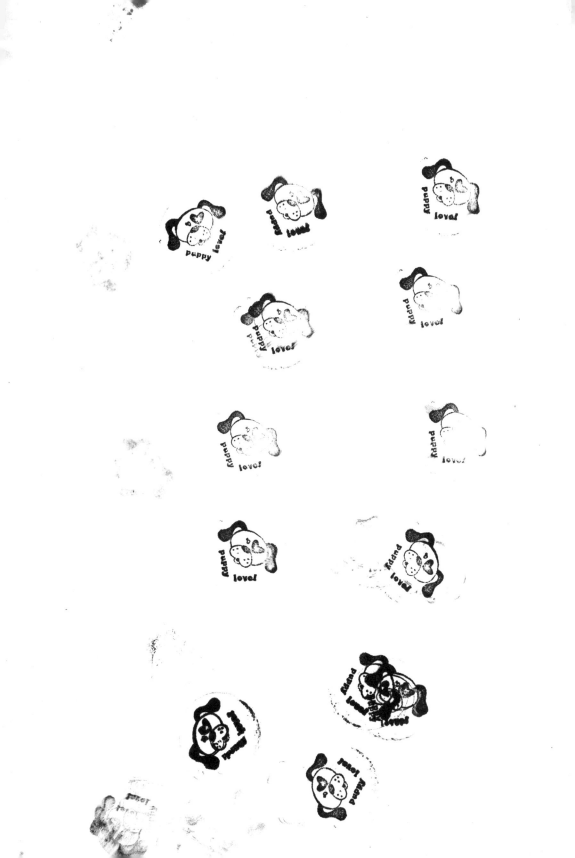

COOL CATS

Ragdolls

by Rebecca Felix

BELLWETHER MEDIA · MINNEAPOLIS, MN

Note to Librarians, Teachers, and Parents:

Blastoff! Readers are carefully developed by literacy experts and combine standards-based content with developmentally appropriate text.

Level 1 provides the most support through repetition of high-frequency words, light text, predictable sentence patterns, and strong visual support.

Level 2 offers early readers a bit more challenge through varied simple sentences, increased text load, and less repetition of high-frequency words.

Level 3 advances early-fluent readers toward fluency through increased text and concept load, less reliance on visuals, longer sentences, and more literary language.

Level 4 builds reading stamina by providing more text per page, increased use of punctuation, greater variation in sentence patterns, and increasingly challenging vocabulary.

Level 5 encourages children to move from "learning to read" to "reading to learn" by providing even more text, varied writing styles, and less familiar topics.

Whichever book is right for your reader, Blastoff! Readers are the perfect books to build confidence and encourage a love of reading that will last a lifetime!

This edition first published in 2016 by Bellwether Media, Inc.

No part of this publication may be reproduced in whole or in part without written permission of the publisher. For information regarding permission, write to Bellwether Media, Inc., Attention: Permissions Department, 5357 Penn Avenue South, Minneapolis, MN 55419.

Library of Congress Cataloging-in-Publication Data

Felix, Rebecca, 1984-
Ragdolls / by Rebecca Felix.
    pages cm. – (Blastoff! Readers. Cool Cats)
  Summary: "Relevant images match informative text in this introduction to ragdoll cats. Intended for students in kindergarten through third grade"– Provided by publisher.
  Audience: Ages 5-8
  Audience: K to grade 3
  Includes bibliographical references and index.
  ISBN 978-1-62617-234-0 (hardcover: alk. paper)
  1. Ragdoll cat–Juvenile literature. I. Title.
  SF449.R34F35 2016
  636.8–dc23
                              2015007122

Table of **Contents**

Ragdolls are a semi-longhaired **breed** of cat.

4

They are big and fluffy.

These friendly cats are
very relaxed.

They go **limp** when picked up.
This makes them look like a
rag doll!

This breed began in California in 1963. There, a woman named Ann Baker **bred** a long-haired white cat with other cats.

California

N
W E
S

Its kittens were sweet and calm.

Baker soon gave other people permission to breed more cats with these **qualities**. These kittens became ragdolls!

This breed has since become very popular.

Big and Fluffy

Ragdoll cats are very large. They are covered in a soft, fluffy **coat**. Some people **compare** it to rabbit fur!

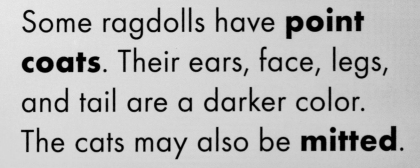

Some ragdolls have **point coats**. Their ears, face, legs, and tail are a darker color. The cats may also be **mitted**.

van coat

Other ragdoll coats are **van** or **bi-color**. Ragdoll colors include chocolate, **lilac**, blue, and **seal**.

Ragdoll Coats

chocolate

lilac

blue

seal

All ragdoll cats have very blue eyes. Their eyes are oval-shaped.

Ragdoll ears are rounded.
They lean forward a little.
The cats' faces are thought to
have sweet expressions.

Ragdoll Profile

—— rounded ears

—— blue eyes

—— large body

—— soft, fluffy hair

Weight: 10 to 20 pounds (5 to 9 kilograms)

Life Span: 12 to 17 years

Ragdoll cats are loving
and **laid-back**.

They flop onto floors or
into their owner's arms.

Ragdolls are sometimes called "puppy-cats." They often meet their owners at the door.

They also follow people around the house. Some ragdoll cats even learn to play fetch!

Glossary

bi-color—a pattern that has two fur colors, one being white

bred—purposely mated two cats to make kittens with certain qualities

breed—a type of cat

coat—the hair or fur covering an animal

compare—to say something is similar to something else

laid-back—calm and relaxed

lilac—a light gray color

limp—soft and weak

mitted—similar to point coats but with white feet, bellies, chins, and necks

point coats—light-colored coats with darker fur in certain areas; pointed cats have dark faces, ears, legs, and tails.

qualities—features that set a breed apart from another

seal—very dark brown

van—a pattern that has dark fur only on the top of the face, ears, and tail, and possibly on a few spots on the body

To Learn More

AT THE LIBRARY

Holland, Gini. *Ragdolls*. New York, N.Y.: PowerKids Press, 2014.

Micco, Trudy. *Discover Ragdoll Cats*. Berkeley Heights, N.J.: Enslow Publishers, 2012.

Stamper, Judith Bauer. *Ragdolls: Alien Cats*. New York, N.Y.: Bearport Pub., 2011.

ON THE WEB

Learning more about ragdoll cats is as easy as 1, 2, 3.

1. Go to www.factsurfer.com.

2. Enter "ragdoll cats" into the search box.

3. Click the "Surf" button and you will see a list of related web sites.

With factsurfer.com, finding more information is just a click away.

Index

The images in this book are reproduced through the courtesy of: Eric Isselee, front cover, pp. 12, 20; Mindy Fawver/ Alamy, p. 4; Erik Lam, pp. 5, 15 (bottom left); Oksana Andersen/ Age Fotostock, p. 6; Domini Brown/ Bellwether Media, p. 7; Labat-Rouquette/ Kimball Stock, p. 9; Juniors Bildarchiv/ Glow Images/ Alamy, pp. 10, 21; Linn Currie, pp. 11, 15 (bottom left); Geoffrey Robinson/ Rex USA/ Newscom, p. 13; silkenphotography, pp. 14, 19; nelik, p. 15 (top left); Tony Campbell, p. 15 (top right); Jonny Kristoffersson, p. 16; Susan Schmitz, p. 17; ChrisRinckes, p. 18.